From Poverty to Prosperity

The Power of Financial Education

Table of Contents

Chapter 1. Introduction

Welcome to an inspiring journey from hardship to abundance, as we present our Special Report titled "From Poverty to Prosperity: The Power of Financial Education." Within these enriching pages, we weave real-life stories of resilience, determination, and most importantly, triumph over adversity. Our journey illuminates how financial literacy can serve as a sturdy bridge, transporting individuals from the depths of poverty to the heights of prosperity. Packed with enlightening interviews, well-researched articles, and expert insights, this report sheds light on the transformative potential of financial education. Discover how knowledge equips individuals with the tools to manage their money diligently, leading to enhanced economic stability and, ultimately, success. A purchase of this special report is an investment in understanding, a beacon guiding towards a prosperous future. Let's take this inspiring leap together!

Chapter 2. The Basics of Financial Education

Financial education, often defined as the ability to understand and use various financial skills including personal financial management, budgeting, and investing, serves as the first step taken on the road to fiscal independence. An understanding of these skills allows people to navigate through financial challenges and opportunities, positioning them not just for survival, but for thriving in an increasingly complex financial environment.

2.1. Financial Literacy: The Foundation

Financial literacy forms the cornerstone of financial education. It involves acquiring knowledge about the fundamental elements of money management such as saving, investing, and using credit wisely. Understanding these elements, and the interplay among them, is essential for building a strong financial future.

People who are financially literate understand how to manage money, how this management contributes to life goals, and how their decisions may impact their financial well-being. For example, in today's world, credit plays a significant role, yet it remains one of the most misunderstood financial aspects. By improving financial literacy, individuals wield the power to use credit as a tool for achieving their financial goals, instead of perceiving it as a burden.

2.2. The Role of Budgeting

Budgeting serves as a roadmap for your financial journey. A budget outlines your income and expenses, giving you an overview of your financial situation. With a budget in place, you can plan for future expenses, identify unnecessary expenses, set realistic goals, and make informed decisions that can help improve your financial stability.

Creating a budget requires discipline, strategic planning, and adherence to certain core principles. First, record your total income and, afterward, list all your expenses. Once you have these details at your disposal, analyze how your expenses align with your income. Finally, prioritize your spending, ensuring basic needs take precedence, and assign funds to savings and investments.

2.3. Understanding Saving and Investing

While often used interchangeably, saving and investing are distinct concepts. Saving is setting aside a portion of your income regularly to meet short-term goals or to serve as an emergency fund. Investing, on the other hand, involves committing money to avenues that offer potential profitable returns. When you invest, you make your money work for you, leading to wealth creation over time.

It's helpful to initiate the savings habit as early as possible. Even modest savings can accumulate into significant amounts over time. The act of saving also encourages discipline and reduces the propensity for frivolous spending.

Investing introduces your money to the power of compounding, where the income from your investments is reinvested to generate additional earnings over time. Different investment options carry different degrees of risk and potential return, so it's important to choose wisely, balancing your financial goals and risk tolerance.

2.4. Credit Management

Using credit wisely is a crucial aspect of financial literacy. Credit enables purchasing power, but when improperly managed, it can lead to debilitating debt. Understanding the cost of credit, including interest rates and charges, aids in making informed borrowing decisions.

Maintain a good credit score to strengthen your bargaining position when negotiating loan terms. Always pay your bills on time and avoid borrowing more than you can afford to repay. Responsible credit use and management not only keep you out of suffocating debt but also boost your financial opportunities and freedom.

2.5. Retirement Planning

You are never too young to start planning for retirement. It should start the moment you begin earning income. A well-planned retirement ensures financial independence when you are no longer in the active workforce.

This planning encompasses forecasting your post-retirement needs and working out a savings and investment strategy to meet those needs. Considerations should include your desired standard of living, potential medical expenses, and inflation. Each of these elements has financial implications that you need to account for in your retirement planning.

To sum up, financial education is a broad field encompassing many topics, concepts, and skills. Yet, all of these concepts mesh to form a cohesive whole – a structured approach to managing your money and making financial decisions with confidence. The journey from poverty to prosperity may not be an easy one, but with financial education, the navigation becomes much simpler and attainable. As you grow in knowledge and understanding, you will learn that you possess the power to define your financial destiny.

This brief overview only scratches the surface of the vast territory that is financial education. A mastery of these basics, however, plants the seeds of financial growth and prosperity. Tend to those seeds, and watch as the landscape of your financial future transforms from one of lack to one of abundance.

Remember, financial knowledge is not just power – it's the power to change lives. Your life. And, ultimately, the world.

Chapter 3. Understanding Poverty: More Than Just Numbers

To comprehend poverty, one must look beyond the numerical definitions imposed by institutions or governments. Indeed, poverty is more than just numerical scarcity. It is a multidimensional phenomenon bridging both financial and non-financial aspects, cascading into the social, cultural, and political lives of individuals and communities.

3.1. Dimensions of Poverty

Poverty is not just economic scarcity. It manifests in various forms ranging from social and political voicelessness and vulnerability to lack of basic services like water, food, housing, and education. It is a web of social disadvantages that significantly curtails and determines the life chances of individuals who don't have the means to break free from it.

The World Bank states that the persistence of poverty stems from three principal causes: lack of access to markets; limited state capacity resulting in poor service provision; and socio-political conflict and violence. Each dimension needs addressing with different solutions, ranging from policy reforms to targeted interventions.

3.2. Measuring Poverty: A Computational Approach

Traditionally, poverty was assessed through a purely monetary lens, using measures such as income or consumption. If a person's income or consumption fell below a certain threshold, defined as the "poverty line," they would be classified as impoverished. Though straightforward in implementation, this unidimensional measurement often fails to capture the full picture of poverty.

The multidimensional poverty index (MPI) developed by United Nations Development Programme (UNDP) and Oxford Poverty and Human Development Initiative (OPHI), offers an expanded view of poverty by taking into consideration various deprivation dimensions like health, education, and standard of living, signifying the scarcity of resources beyond just money.

3.3. Poverty and Exclusion

Poverty holds the power to exclude individuals from their communities, limiting their economic opportunities and stifling their voices. Social exclusion amplifies poverty's impact and makes it more challenging to break free from the poverty trap.

Take, for instance, the case of healthcare. Studies show that the financially poor are often the last to access medical amenities despite their higher chances of experiencing health problems. In part, this results from their inability to afford medical expenses. Consequently, the economic strain on those in poverty heightens further, pushing them deeper into the vicious cycle.

3.4. Education and Poverty

Education is often dubbed the 'great equalizer', necessary in escalating one's socio-economic standing. However, individuals living in poverty often face significant barriers to education, such as the lack of access to quality schooling, structural and systemic discrimination, or the sheer need for surviving, which takes precedence over acquiring an education.

Yet, when given the chance, education can reverse the tide of poverty. Education, more often than not, leads to increased earning potentials, better health, and an improved quality of life. The investment in education may initially seem tedious, particularly when dealing with immediate survival needs, but the long-term benefits it yields are substantial.

3.5. Toward Poverty Alleviation

Understanding poverty as more than just numbers compels us to scrutinize solutions beyond mere income redistribution. While financial aid and welfare programs play crucial roles in providing immediate relief, they are often insufficient for long-term poverty alleviation.

It is here that financial education seizes the stage. By equipping individuals with fiscal literacy, we empower them to better manage their finances, stimulate their earning potential, and even navigate towards financial independence. Our subsequent chapters explore these facets of financial education at length, shedding light on how it serves as a sturdy bridge, leading from the depths of poverty to the heights of prosperity.

In conclusion, poverty, being more than just a state of being poor, is a complex, multifaceted issue. Understanding and addressing poverty requires comprehensive efforts that attack the root causes while also combating its effects. Such considerations are essential to developing effective, sustainable strategies to alleviate poverty.

Chapter 4. How Knowledge Transforms Destinies

There's an adage that knowledge is power. This becomes especially true when we delve into the world of finance. From learning to manage a simple savings account to comprehend the complex entanglements of investments and debts, the journey of acquiring financial literacy can mean the difference between a life of struggle and a future of prosperity. In this chapter, we explore how gaining - and applying - knowledge can significantly transform destinies, ultimately leading individuals from the clutches of poverty to the realms of financial success.

4.1. The Significance of Financial Literacy

Understanding personal finance is rarely given its due credit, often times dismissed as concepts reserved for bankers or economists. However, the truth is that financial literacy extends far beyond Wall Street. It is a fundamental life skill, and the lack of it can have far-reaching consequences. An individual's financial literacy level can impact their quality of life, ability to fulfill basic needs, secure their futures, and even influence their mental and physical health.

Studies show a direct correlation between the level of an individual's financial literacy and their economic prosperity. According to a survey by the TIAA Institute, individuals with high financial literacy are more likely to plan for retirement, an act that has been linked with higher wealth levels.

Financial literacy also plays a significant role in reducing the anxiety associated with money management. Research indicates that people with a low level of financial literacy tend to have a higher level of financial stress, which can negatively impact their overall well-being. By imparting the knowledge required to manage and grow wealth, financial education is key to empowering individuals, lifting them from a life of hardship, and introducing them to a world where they can chase their dreams without the constant worry of living paycheck to paycheck.

4.2. The Transformative Role of Education

Education often serves as a catalyst in turning the tide of financial well-being. The effects are more visible and profound when education transcends traditional subjects and ventures into the realm of personal finance. Simply put, financial education can fundamentally shift the trajectory of individuals trapped in a cycle of poverty and provide them with an actionable path to economic independence.

A critical aspect of this transformation revolves around the fundamentals of budgeting. Financial education unravels the mysteries of income and expenditure, making individuals aware of their spending habits, necessary expenses, and the importance of saving. Once this knowledge is applied, individuals are empowered to take control of their finances, leading to more informed decisions regarding spending and saving.

Additionally, financial education introduces concepts like investing and wealth growth. It's no secret that wealthier individuals usually have investments that generate income, rather than relying solely on salaries or wages. By explaining the basics of investing and showcasing the potential results, financial education offers a real, tangible way towards prosperity.

4.3. Knowledge Enabling the Conquering of Debt

One of the crippling challenges faced by individuals in poverty is the issue of debt. Here again, financial education plays a pivotal role in combating this problem. It provides the necessary tools to strategically manage and gradually eliminate debt.

Financial literacy programs do this by teaching individuals how to prioritize their debts, focus on high-interest ones, and balance out their incomes and expenses, thus carving out funds for repayment. Knowing how much, when, and where to repay becomes a strategy instead of a burden. As Abraham Lincoln wisely said, "Give me six hours to chop down a tree, and I will spend the first four sharpening the ax." Thus, equipping one's self with financial literacy is the sharpening needed to conquer the towering tree of debt.

4.4. Case Studies: Turning Knowledge into Action

Perhaps the most powerful demonstration of the transformative impact of financial knowledge are real-life success stories. For instance, there's the case of Jane, a single mother who lived paycheck to paycheck. By enrolling in a financial literacy program, she learned to budget, save, and eventually enrolled in a community college to enhance her earnings.

Then there's John, a college student with mounting student loans. After attending personal finance workshops, he learned about managing debts and planning for repayment. Now, he's well on his way to becoming debt-free while having a secure job in his field of study. Such stories reinforce the fact that financial knowledge, when applied in real-life, has transformative potential.

This chapter serves as a testament to the power of financial education. It reaffirms the belief that knowledge, when acquired and applied right, has the power to drastically improve the financial health of individuals. An understanding of financial concepts equips people with the right tools, enabling them to make informed decisions, effectively manage their wealth, and break free from the cycle of poverty. Financial knowledge is indeed a formidable tool in transforming destinies, leading to a future glistening with possibilities of prosperity.

Chapter 5. Money Management: Core Principles and Tools

Prudent money management is akin to building a sturdy foundation for a house. It enables individuals to strategically navigate fiscal landscapes, mitigate economic uncertainties, and propels them towards financial wellness. Despite its critical nature, there's a looming gap in our understanding of the basic principles and tools that govern money management. This chapter aims to fill that void, offering profound insights into mastering the art of managing finances successfully.

5.1. Budgeting: An Essential Start

Budgeting can be likened to a road map, guiding our financial decisions and showcasing the route to our goals. Making and adhering to a budget calls for discipline, punctuality, and patience - but the rewards far outweigh the effort.

A well-structured budget can significantly enhance money management by helping individuals track income and expenses, foresee financial challenges, and make informed decisions about savings and investments. Here are several vital components of an effective budget:

- Income: The first step is identifying your total income, including wages, salaries, returns from investments, financial gifts, and other sources.

- Expenses: This involves tracking all outgoing cash flows, such as rent, utility bills, groceries, entertainment, travel, and healthcare costs.

- Savings Goals: Based on the income and expenses, set realistic short and long-term savings goals.

- Debt Repayment: Any existing debts should be incorporated into the budget, with a focus on reducing and eventually eliminating the debt burden.

5.2. Understand the Power of Compound Interest

Albert Einstein once referred to compound interest as "the eighth wonder of the world.' Understanding it is vital for successful money management, as it can work either in favor or against you.

Compound interest refers to earning (or owing) interest on both the initial sum and its accumulated interest over time. For instance, when saving or investing, the money grows exponentially because interest is earned on the amount which is continually increasing. However, on loans or credit cards, more interest is accrued over time, which is why it's important to pay off these debts as quickly as possible.

5.3. Tools for Money Management

In today's dynamic digital era, several online tools and apps aid in efficient money management. Here are a few noteworthy ones:

1. Budgeting Apps: Tools like Mint, YNAB (You Need a Budget), and PocketGuard help users track their expenses, create budgets, and even offer personalized tips for saving.

2. Investment Apps: Platforms like Acorns, Stash, and Robinhood make the investment process easier while providing valuable insight into the current market trends.

3. Debt Tracker Apps: These tools, such as Debt Payoff Planner and

Unbury.Me, aid users in planning their debt repayment and tracking their progress.

5.4. Managing Credit Wisely

Credit management is a crucial aspect of financial well-being. It involves understanding your credit score, using credit cards judiciously, and maintaining a good credit history for future financial needs like home loans or car loans.

5.5. Emergency Funds: The Financial Airbag

The third key element of money management is setting up an emergency fund - a treasure chest of savings reserved for unexpected life events such as job loss, car repairs, or medical emergencies. Financial experts typically recommend keeping three to six months' worth of living expenses in an easily accessible bank account.

5.6. The Habit of Saving

When it comes to financial well-being, saving isn't just an act - it's a habit. Whether it's stashing money away for a major purchase, setting up an emergency fund, or investing for retirement, the act of saving pushes you toward your future goals.

Remember, it's not about how much you save, but the consistency with which you do it. Even small monthly contributions can add up significantly over time due to the power of compound interest and regular investing.

Navigating the path to financial prosperity requires comprehension and application of these core principles and tools of money management. By adopting these practices, individuals can attain economic stability, alleviate poverty, and leap towards abundance. Through financial education, you are not just ensuring your personal growth, but also contributing to the overall economic prosperity of your community.

In our endeavor to foster financial literacy, the journey from 'poverty to prosperity' continues, shedding light on more critical aspects of financial education in the subsequent segments of this report.

Chapter 6. Real Stories of Transformation

Beginning this incredible journey, we reflect on the lives of those who've traced the path from poverty to prosperity, underscoring the immense power and transformative potential of financial education.

6.1. Overcoming Barriers: The Story of John

John was born into a family crushed beneath the weight of poverty. The eldest of five children, John grappled with deprivation, impotent to change his family's dire circumstances. Unwilling to resign himself to his destined life-course, he pursued financial education against all odds.

Armed with a local library card, John began by consuming every piece of financial literature he could get his hands on. Day by day, financial concepts that were once shrouded in mystery became more transparent and accessible. With this newfound understanding, John not only managed to escape the poverty trap but also made ample provisions for a secure future for himself and his family.

6.2. Turning Tides: Laura's Resilience

Laura was a single mother stuck in a toxic job, forced to borrow money just to keep the lights on. She was living hand-to-mouth, drowning in debts with interest rates escalating beyond comprehension. But a chance encounter at her child's school would change the course of her life forever.

At a PTA meeting, Laura was introduced to a financial literacy initiative, offering courses and resources to adults. Seeing a beacon of hope, Laura began investing her scanty free hours into absorbing financial education. Trading ignorance for comprehension, Laura learned discerning methods to manage her income, save despite limited resources, and turn her liabilities into an asset powerhouse, one strategic step at a time.

6.3. A Late Blossom: Granny Smith's Second Chance

A staunch advocate for financial literacy today, Granny Smith, at the age of 75, was once coerced to embrace an impoverished life. Having lost her partner, she floated aimlessly in the ocean of financial uncertainty until the local community center began offering free introductory financial literacy classes.

Inspired by the promise of newfound independence, Smith enthusiastically took up the course, despite her age and debilitating ailments. Unfazed by her initial struggles, Smith learned the importance of budgeting, the practice of investing, and how to create and maintain an emergency fund. Now, not only is she a financially independent, retired septuagenarian, but also a vocal advocate for financial literacy amongst her peers.

6.4. A Tale of Empowerment: Maya's Revolution

The story of Maya—an underprivileged, uneducated housemaid—stands testimony to the revolutionary potential of financial education. Following the path sketched out by her societal status, Maya seemed doomed to perpetual poverty until her employer, an economist, offered her a life-changing proposition: a financial education.

Maya accepted, and the ensuing months of relentless dedication brought about a sea change in her life's trajectory. Concepts like savings, budgeting, and investing in mutual funds, once alien, became the guiding pillars of her financial existence. Today, Maya not only lives debt-free but also comfortably supports her children's education.

6.5. The Phoenix Rises: Raymond's Resurrection

Declared bankrupt at the mere age of 27 and seemingly incarcerated in a perpetual debt cycle, Raymond stands as a beacon of hope for people experiencing financial distress. Raymond's turning point came when he stumbled upon a financial literacy course while searching for job opportunities online.

Raymond took to the lessons like a moth to a flame, sifting through credit management, budgeting, savings, investing, and more. His transformation was strictly incremental, erasing debts, incorporating savings, and undertaking low-risk investments. Today, Raymond is a self-made millionaire and a motivational financial educator, avidly propagating the principles of financial literacy.

Through these stories, one fact resonates—irrespective of circumstances, age, or societal standing, financial education is unequivocally transformational. No story is too trivial, no transformation insignificant. Financial literacy equips each one with the power to dictate their financial future responsibly, unfettered by the chains of societal or economic determinants. This extraordinary journey through real-life transformations is testimony to the transformative potential of financial literacy.

Chapter 7. The Role of Financial Literacy in Developing Economies

Economic stability often feels beyond reach in developing countries. Poverty, corruption, and instability cast long shadows. Yet, financial literacy presents a transformative opportunity under these trying circumstances. The dissemination of this crucial knowledge is invaluable, equipping individuals with the skills required to break free from the crippling cycle of poverty.

7.1. The Importance of Financial Literacy

Financial literacy, defined as the ability to understand and effectively apply various financial skills, including personal financial management, budgeting, and investing, offers a path to self-sufficiency. It serves as an essential instrument towards promoting economic stability, growth, and diminished poverty levels. Further, it provides individuals with the tools necessary to understand financial risk and allows them to plan for the future, protect their earnings, and take advantage of opportunities to grow their wealth.

Disseminating financial literacy equips individuals with the knowledge required to transcend the poverty line and participate more fully in their economy. From navigating banking systems and understanding loan interest, to making informed choices about savings, entrepreneurship, and investments, financial literacy benefits both individuals and their larger communities.

7.2. The State of Financial Literacy in Developing Economies

In developing economies, access to financial education is often limited. Those living in poverty generally have low levels of education and literacy, leaving them ill-equipped to handle financial matters. Systemic issues like limited access to financial institutions and poorly developed financial infrastructures exacerbate the issue.

Results from the Standard & Poor's Ratings Services Global Financial Literacy Survey indicate that in major economies, like South Africa, India, and Brazil, only 13%–31% of adults are financially literate. A more alarming observation is that the marginalized sections, such as the elderly, women, and rural communities, rate even lower.

In sharp contrast, developed economies like Australia, Canada, and the UK project a far greater percentage of financially literate adults, between 57% to 70%.

7.3. Incorporating Financial Literacy into Educational Systems

One solution to this challenge lies in early education. Incorporating comprehensive financial literacy programs into school curricula from a young age could equip young people with the tools they need to manage finances effectively, thereby empowering them to make informed decisions in the future.

For instance, the non-profit Aflatoun offers social and financial education to children and young people in more than 100 countries, helping them to save, budget, and invest, fostering entrepreneurship skills and promoting social change.

While teachers themselves often lack this previously overlooked knowledge, increasing resources, and international focus on the matter mean more opportunities for teacher training, ensuring this vital information reaches the classroom.

7.4. Enhancing Financial Literacy Through Technology

Emerging technology serves as another powerful tool in combatting financial ignorance in developing countries. Mobile banking, digital finance apps, and online learning platforms provide modern and accessible ways to spread essential financial knowledge.

Digital platforms have the potential to reach rural and low-income groups who traditionally have limited access to traditional banking systems or formal financial training. M-Pesa, a mobile money transfer service in Kenya, has revolutionized banking in Africa by providing access to money transfer and banking services, even in remote locations. It also offers a platform for financial literacy efforts.

7.5. The Role of Government and Non-Governmental Organizations (NGOs)

The government and NGOs play an indispensable part in promoting financial literacy. By implementing policies that ensure access to financial education is widespread and accessible, they can facilitate society's vulnerable sections.

Specific initiatives, like India's National Strategy for Financial Education or Tanzania's National Financial Education Framework, tackle the issue head-on, targeting a diverse range of demographics, including school children, rural communities, and the elderly.

Non-Governmental Organizations also play a pivotal role. Institutions like the Financial Literacy Initiative Foundation in Zambia and the Global Financial Literacy Excellence Center in the USA work arduously to make financial education accessible, often reaching marginalized communities overlooked by traditional efforts.

7.6. The Impact of Financial Literacy on Poverty and Development

The empowerment that comes from financial literacy cannot be overstated. While short-term benefits may include increased savings or successful loan repayments, the long-term potential is even more abundant.

Evidence suggests that financial literacy not only staves off personal financial disaster but can also drive significant economic benefits, increasing entrepreneurship, job creation, and economic growth. When a significant portion of the population in a developing country becomes financially literate, a significant impact on the national economy follows.

As an illustration, a study by The World Bank on India found that financial literacy programs improved financial planning and household wellbeing, indicative of apparent monetary growth at the household level, propagating the potential trickle-up effect into national economics.

In conclusion, financial literacy, when effectively disseminated and implemented, can be a powerful tool for economic development. Notwithstanding the barriers, the enduring efforts of governments, NGOs, educational institutions, and digital platforms can pave the way towards increased economic stability in developing countries, fostering an environment conducive to pushing the boundaries of human potential.

Chapter 8. Education Programs Making a Difference

In the arena of prosperity, education, particularly financial education, plays an unparalleled role. As such, various education programs around the globe are radically transforming the financial landscape through their robust curricula and empowering initiatives. Through this chapter, we delve into the journey of these programs, their impact, and the determined individuals behind them.

8.1. Embracing the Challenge: Bridging Financial Literacy Gap

The challenges in delivering proper financial education are multi-pronged. First and foremost is the lack of knowledge and resources in disadvantaged communities. Then, there's the problem of making financial literacy appealing and accessible — a daunting task often met with resistance due to the seemingly complex nature of financial terms and concepts. To overcome these hurdles, a batch of initiatives has been developed.

A prime example of such initiatives is "Bridging the Financial Literacy Gap" (BFLG), a program that targets one of the most financially vulnerable demographics — young adults. Equipping these young minds with early financial knowledge, the BFLG program paves the way for financially stable adulthood. The program includes an extensive course on budgeting, savings, and investment — essentials that are seldom taught in schools. It offers its content in an engaging, digestible format, making the learning process relatable and enjoyable.

8.2. Banking on Change: Delivering Financial Education in Rural Areas

In rural arenas where formal banking is often an alien concept, financial education presents an unparalleled challenge. Nevertheless, "Banking on Change" (BOC) is a remarkable initiative that has turned the tide. Exploiting the power of technology, BOC delivers financial education to the remotest corners of the world.

Through an advanced mobile application, the initiative delivers basic lessons on savings, credit, and digital transactions. Moreover, BOC also organizes practical workshops in local languages, allowing a more tactile understanding of financial concepts. Their hands-on approach has more than doubled the number of rural individuals utilizing formal banking services, validating the efficacy of their strategies.

8.3. Money Mentorship: Fostering Financial Responsibility Among Children

Believing that financial education should be imparted at an early age, the "Money Mentorship" campaign has designed a unique program catered to children as young as seven. The program builds on the premise that children are not merely passive recipients but active economic agents.

The curriculum introduces money management through enjoyable activities and stimulating games. Furthermore, it engages parents, too, shedding light on how to cultivate good money habits in their children. Their work has helped foster a generation of financially capable children, emphasizing the importance of financial literacy from a tender age.

8.4. Financial Pathways: Tackling Poverty Through Microfinancing

While financial knowledge is crucial, it also needs to be complemented by financial opportunities, which is where "Financial Pathways" excels. Addressing the poor access to finance in distressed regions, this program integrates microfinancing with financial education.

The beneficiaries, primarily women, are offered small loans to start businesses. Along with this, they receive training on managing finances, savings, and repayments. This dual strategy has signaled a significant fall in the default rates, demonstrating that financial knowledge truly impacts financial behavior.

8.5. Tech Empower: Digitally Breaking Financial Boundaries

"Tech Empower," a tech-based initiative, has embraced the digital revolution to spread financial literacy. Creating a compelling blend of technology and finance, Tech Empower leverages virtual reality, gamification, and A.I. to turn financial education into a captivating experience.

Their groundbreaking applications have proven that learning finance can be an exciting venture, overcoming resistance to dull theoretical learning. With an emphasis on cyber finance, cybersecurity, and digital transactions, "Tech Empower" is a frontrunner in revolutionizing financial education among digital natives.

Through their unwavering commitment, these educational programs, and numerous others, are creating ripples of change, orchestrating a symphony of financial transformation that echoes from an individual to the global level. These efforts have fortified faith in education's power, demonstrating that financial literacy is indeed a propelling force from poverty to prosperity. With their robust initiatives, the era of financial empowerment is not too distant. The next sections will delve deeper into the financial struggles faced by individuals and how they've been overcome, paving the way for us to further appreciate these groundbreaking educational courses.

Chapter 9. Policy Interventions: Shaping the Future of Financial Education

Financial education represents more than just knowledge; it's a life-changing tool that enables individuals to build stable futures. It provides the stepping stones to transform lives from deprivation to prosperity. Policymakers have a crucial role in shaping this transformative potential of financial education.

9.1. The Role of Policy in Financial Literacy

The first step toward cultivating actionable polic strategies is understanding the significance of financial education and how policy can nurture it. Education policies can serve to enhance public financial literacy, leading to economic resilience amongst the masses. Effective policy-making, then, necessitates a comprehensive understanding of the state of financial education and the pitfalls that hinder its progress.

In addition to establishing measures for immediate improvement, policy interventions need to consider long-term sustainability. This involves regular evaluation and necessary adjustments of current policies. Large-scale financial education drives, when complemented with effective policies, can significantly impact societal economic advancement.

9.2. Promoting Inclusive Financial Education

An inclusive financial education curriculum encourages learning across diverse age groups and income brackets. Ensuring this universality necessitates policies that don't just cater to the school-age population but also adults who missed out on these lessons during their formative years. Special focus has to be laid upon marginalized groups, including low-income families and immigrants, who suffer due to poor access to financial literacy.

Policy measures must focus on eliminating socio-economic barriers that obstruct access to financial education. This can involve government and non-profit initiatives aimed at expanding the scope of financial literacy programs to reach these marginalized groups.

9.3. Ensuring Quality of Financial Education

While outreach is important, policymakers must ensure that the quality of education imparted is exceptional and contextually relevant. Policies should outline the core competencies that a well-rounded financial literacy program should cover. These might include basics such as understanding interest rates, the importance of saving, elements of budgeting, and identifying financial frauds.

Emphasizing the quality of financial literacy programs also translates into accrediting educators and validating educational resources. Policies should define a benchmark for educators' skills and qualifications to maintain a standardized level of teaching across all platforms.

9.4. Collaborative Efforts and Partnerships

The potential of policy influence transcends boundaries of public bodies and extends to private sectors and non-profit organizations. These collaborations can capitalize on the expertise and resources each sector brings, orchestrating holistic financial literacy initiatives.

A harmonious partnership can tap into the corporate world's resources and non-profit organizations' grassroots reach to ensure a broader dissemination of financial knowledge. Such alliances often lead to robust financial education programs, often fostering financial independence in communities.

9.5. Leveraging Technology for Financial Education

Digital platforms offer an effective avenue for promoting financial literacy, particularly amidst the millennial and Gen Z population. Policy directives can advocate for the innovative use of technology in delivering financial education. This may involve incorporating financial literacy in digital games, developing AI-driven learning tools, or harnessing the power of mobile apps.

9.6. Monitoring, Evaluation, and Continuous Improvements

Just as financial education is a continuous journey, policies that drive it need to demonstrate the same flexibility and readiness to evolve. Regular assessments should be etched into these policies, which can provide important insights into the effectiveness of existing efforts.

Above all, it's crucial to remember that the impact of financial education cannot materialize overnight. Patience, persistence, and a steadfast commitment to introducing reforms where needed are key.

Policymakers are indeed the architects of broad-based financial literacy initiatives. Their role extends much beyond drafting laws and extends to shaping a future that thrives on the power of financial education. Through inclusive, quality-driven policy interventions that promote collaborations, leverage technology and advocate constant improvements, a future of financial prosperity becomes an achievable reality rather than a distant dream.

Chapter 10. Businesses Empowering Through Financial Literacy

Reducing financial illiteracy is not only the duty of individuals or the government; corporations also have a crucial role to play in promoting monetary understanding. Businesses of varying scale—from multinational corporations to small enterprises—are committing resources to improve financial literacy, understanding that it contributes to overall economic health and, ultimately, benefits everyone.

10.1. An Introduction to Financial Literacy Programs

Businesses implementing financial literacy programs recognize the importance of a financially aware staff. They consider it a necessary step towards contributing to their overall success, not just as monetary gain, but by creating a robust and resilient economic environment conducive to positive growth.

Global banking giant, Goldman Sachs, for instance, introduced the '10,000 Women' initiative. This program offers practical business education, mentoring and networking, and access to capital for female entrepreneurs. The '10,000 Women' program has reached participants from over 56 countries and drastically improved the recipients' business revenue and employment generation.

Similarly, Mastercard runs the 'Girls4Tech' program aiming to drive interest towards the subjects of science, technology, engineering and math (STEM) and finance-based careers for girls aged between 8-12 years. Since the program's initiation in 2014, Girls4Tech has reached multiple countries worldwide, highlighting the universal need to address female financial illiteracy.

10.2. Corporations Inspiring Change

One of the key elements of these financial literacy programs is their potential to instigate significant transformations in both organizations and employees' lives. When a large corporation promotes financial literacy, its influence reaches beyond immediate staff, trickling down to affect suppliers, clients, and even the community at large.

Visa's Practical Money Skills initiative demonstrates a profound effect. This long-standing financial education resource provides educators, parents, and students access to free educational resources. Not only does Visa's program improve participants' financial skills, it also promotes a culture of monetary responsibility and diligence.

Starbucks is renowned for its commitment towards its employees (or 'partners,' as they are called internally). Their comprehensive benefits program includes access to financial planning tools and resources. The initiative is rooted in the firm belief that in order to serve customers to the best of their ability, the individuals behind Starbucks need to be satisfied, secure, and financially informed.

10.3. The Microfinance Model and Financial Literacy

Often, large corporations are not the only players that make a significant impact. Microfinance institutions (MFIs) can also drive positive change, as they directly target low-income individuals who might lack access to conventional banking services.

Grameen Bank, a microfinance organization and community development bank founded in Bangladesh, incorporates a unique model. It emphasizes financial education as a fundamental part of its lending process. Before clients can receive loans, they must partake in intensive training sessions focusing on money management and entrepreneurship. The bank's comprehensive approach ensures recipients understand the terms of their loans, how to utilize these funds, and most importantly, how to repay them on time. This preventive measure tackles the problem of over-indebtedness from its roots, giving the borrowers a much better chance at financial success.

10.4. The Win-Win Situation

Businesses that invest in financial literacy education often see returns on their investment extending far beyond altruistic factors. When employees understand personal finance, they build a stable economic situation. This stability often translates into improved performance at work, as financially secure employees contribute to the productivity and positive aura in the workplace.

Moreover, a ripple effect is created in the community. As more people understand the significance of sound financial planning and practices, they improve their lifespan's economic health. This holistic transformation impacts an entire generation, raising the community's overall standard of living.

By promoting financial literacy, businesses can make a profound impact on their employees' lives, strengthen the community's economic resilience, fulfill their corporate social responsibility and contribute to sustainable development goals. The journey from poverty to prosperity may be long, but it is undeniably impactful. Financial education paves the path towards economic empowerment, helping individuals transcend adversity, and businesses are playing an essential role in constructing this bridge strengthened with knowledge and understanding. The stories contained herein provide a testament to the strength, resilience, and enduring power of financial literacy. They inspire us to continue working to create a world equipped with the financial education necessary to break the cycle of poverty.

Chapter 11. The Road Ahead: Sustaining Prosperity Through Financial Education

Financial education, a powerful tool, stands at the precipitous peak of struggle and success, poverty and prosperity. This particular component of knowledge, often overlooked in conventional instructional designs, is the very foundation upon which financial independence is built.

11.1. A Golden Key: The Power of Financial Education

Many follow the traditional pathway of school, employment, savings and, finally the purchase of a house – an embodiment of stability and success. However, economic constancy often reaches a precarious equilibrium when faced with real-world challenges. It is in these instances that an understanding of personal finance and money management becomes invaluable.

Financial education equips individuals with insights into complex economic concepts, from the fundamental (understanding profits, losses, loans and savings) to the complex (investments, taxes, and retirement planning). Armed with this understanding, people are capable of making informed decisions that impact not just the trajectory of their lives, but the socio-economic fabric of entire communities.

11.2. Elevation from Financial Illiteracy: A Daunting Challenge

Regrettably, financial illiteracy remains a pervasive global issue. More often than not, those raised in monetary insufficiency lack the opportunity to explore the convolutions of fiscal management. Most educational systems worldwide largely ignore this crucial aspect of learning, resulting in generations of financially naïve adults.

The world is not kind to the uninformed. In this complex ecosystem of finance, without a clear comprehension of personal finances, individuals unknowingly stumble upon debt traps and usurious loans, accelerating their descent into poverty. Financial education is a vital stepping stone for these individuals to step out of the vicious cycle of debt and poverty and step onto an ascension ladder to prosperity and success.

11.3. The Promise of Personal Financial Management

At the core of financial education is personal financial management. It configures an individual's approach towards earnings, savings, expenditure, and investments.

Rather than readily succumbing to instant gratification or the allure of reckless investments, financial education prompts individuals to meticulously plan and adhere to a budget. Such practices methodically direct income towards savings, eventually paving the way for investments which, in turn, form a passive income stream - a powerful cushion against potential financial downturns.

11.4. Compass for Investment: Navigating the Economic Ocean

Investing is both a science and an art that can feel daunting to the uninitiated. However, for those with a strong grounding in financial education, it represents an avenue for economic growth and financial independence beyond regular income. The stock market, mutual funds, real estate, bonds – all come with their risks and returns. The key here is to diversify, maintain a long-term perspective and not to be swayed by short-term market fluctuations.

Financial education trains individuals to 'ride the tide' rather than be engulfed by it. For those who understand the intricate dance of investment, the prospect of multiplying wealth is not just a dream, but a tangible reality.

11.5. The Impact on Quality of Life: The Long-term Effects

Good money habits influence all aspects of life, significantly improving its quality. Saving for a child's education, planning for a comfortable retirement, purchasing a house – all these previously intimidating milestones become achievable targets with robust financial planning. Significantly, this alleviates an enormous amount of stress and contributes towards mental well-being.

Financial education is also the key to fostering economic equality. Empowering the underprivileged with financial knowledge helps shrink income disparity, thus contributing to a more balanced society.

11.6. Road Ahead: A Call to Action

The road ahead is clear - financial literacy is not an option; it is a necessity. While governments and educational bodies worldwide have increasingly detailed financial literacy in their curriculums, it is not enough. Non-profits and corporate entities need to pitch in with their resources, conducting workshops and implementing programs to enhance financial awareness.

Also, it is essential to remember that the benefits of financial education aren't limited to the individual alone. When we lift people from the depths of poverty, we elevate society with them. The chain effect of this social upliftment is tremendous and helps us foster a more equitable and resilient world.

In conclusion, the journey from poverty to prosperity is fraught with challenges, reprieve, and life-altering decisions. But with financial education functioning as the compass, the road to prosperity no longer seems treacherous. Instead, it serves as a journey of self-discovery, triumph, and eventual prosperity. The road ahead, though laden with challenges, is a path of promise and potential, thanks to the power of financial education.